A DAY IN THE LIFE OF A
Photographer

Text and photographs by Gayle Jann

Troll Associates

Library of Congress Cataloging in Publication Data

Jann, Gayle.
    A day in the life of a photographer.

    Summary: Follows a free-lance photographer through
his day as he sets up his schedule and fulfills a variety
of photographic assignments.
      1. Reichert, Robert—Juvenile literature.   2. Photo-
graphers—United States—Biography—Juvenile literature.
3. Photography—Vocational guidance—Juvenile literature.
[1. Photographers. 2. Occupations. 3. Reichert, Robert]
I. Title.
TR140.R37   1988   770'.92'4   87-13751
ISBN 0-8167-1123-2 (lib. bdg.)
ISBN 0-8167-1124-0 (pbk.)

The author and publisher wish to thank Robert Reichert for his generous gift of time and input to this project. Thanks also to John Santoro of Brecker & Merryman, Inc. (Human Resource Consulting Firm). Photographs on pages 9, 24, 26 and 28 © Robert Reichert.

Robert Reichert is a free-lance photographer. He sets his own schedule, so each day on the job is different from the one before. Robert often gets up early so he can take photographs in the golden light of the sunrise. Light is a photographer's most important tool.

Competition among photographers is very strong. That's why Robert always looks for new and exciting ways to photograph both common and unusual subjects. The city skyline is a popular subject for photographers. Building goes on all the time and the skyline is constantly changing.

Robert's schedule is very busy, so he keeps track of his assignments in an appointment book. Often his clients reserve time far in advance. A day or two before each assignment, Robert calls his client to make sure there have been no changes in the schedule and the "shoot" will take place on the day he has reserved.

Robert has a mailing list of clients he has worked for in the past and companies he would like to work for in the future. He keeps in touch with them by sending out promotional mailings. His wife, Melinda, who also acts as his representative, helps Robert select samples of his best and most interesting work to include in the mailing.

Melinda also helps keep Robert's portfolio up to date by looking through magazines that have used his photographs. She cuts out "tear sheets" and adds them to Robert's portfolio, which will be shown to design firms and corporations. By looking at the portfolio, prospective clients can see a variety of Robert's work.

A client may need one photo, or several. However, a photographer usually shoots many rolls of film, using different camera angles, exposures, and lighting effects. Then the best shots are submitted. Today, Robert selects 50 shots from hundreds of recent photos. He likes to keep his portfolio as current as possible.

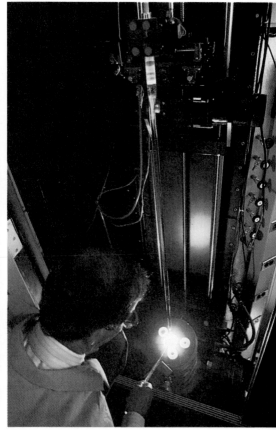

Robert is skilled at making dramatic and unusual photographs. He selects for his portfolio some slides he took for a trade magazine. He created an exciting image using lights with color filters, plus light from the client's machine. The machine in the photo makes fiber optics, which are used in communications.

Many pictures appear to be similar. But the right
expression, gesture, angle, or shadow can make
the difference between an average shot and a very
special photograph. Robert must be a critical
judge of his own work. He marks the "contact
sheets" with a red grease pencil when he decides
which shots he will enlarge and print.

Black and white photographic paper is sensitive to white light but not to dim red or amber light. In the darkroom, Robert works under a 15-watt red or amber "safe light." Before he puts the negative into the enlarger, he checks the negative, which is in a "negative carrier." He must make sure there is no dust on it.

To make a print, three different chemicals are needed—developer, stop and fixer. Each chemical must be drained from the print before the print is put into the next chemical. After the print has been in the fixer for a few minutes, the white lights can be turned on. Finally, the print will be washed.

As a free-lance photographer, Robert is in business for himself. He does his own billing, and keeps careful records of his fees and expenses. He checks to see that his invoices were mailed, and he notes all of his expenses in his record-keeping ledgers. He has learned that business skills are necessary if you want to be your own boss.

Robert often photographs "on location." Today he is shooting photographs for a brochure for a food company. He and his client's project director arrive together. For location shooting, Robert often takes along a variety of equipment. He uses lights and special lenses to help create interesting photographs. First he adjusts the curtains that will be the background for this shot.

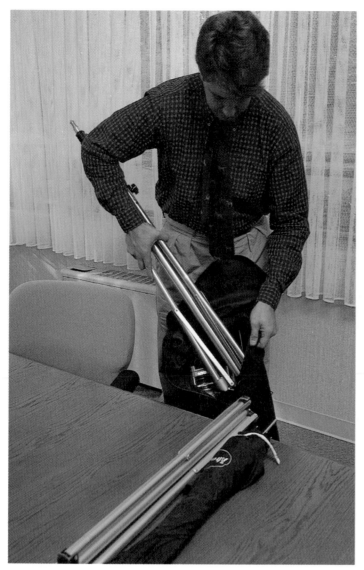

Robert begins setting up the lights he has brought along. First he opens up the stand that will hold the lights. Sometimes Robert wants the light to bounce off a white umbrella. This gives a soft but somewhat directional light that is desirable for certain kinds of photographs.

Sometimes just a reflector is used, and the light is bounced off the ceiling or a wall. This will spread the light in many directions, for a softer effect in the photograph. Before the shoot begins, Robert cleans the camera lens carefully. A dirty lens could mean a loss of sharpness in a photograph.

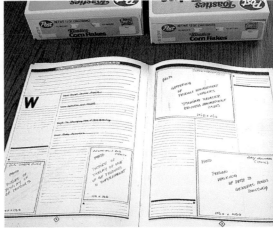

Robert discusses with the client how the photograph he is taking will be used in the brochure. Robert sometimes works with a "layout," or a design of what the brochure page will look like. The layout may show whether the photograph should be vertical, horizontal, or cropped to a square format.

Correct exposure of the film is critical to a successful shot. Robert takes an exposure reading with a light meter. When he presses the button, the meter will indicate the proper setting for Robert's lens. To double check the lighting, Robert takes a Polaroid shot with the same setting.

Robert and his client look at the Polaroid. They must decide whether or not they want to make changes before Robert takes the photograph. The Polaroid shows things that are hard to notice with the naked eye. For example, if the lights have not been placed correctly, their reflection in the windows could ruin the shot.

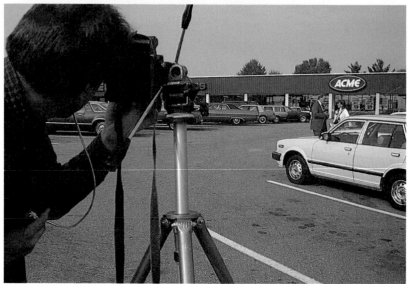

The client also wants Robert to take other photographs of the same people. Robert will be shooting outdoors, with a supermarket for the background. He takes a reading with a light meter and selects a different exposure. Outdoors, photographers usually work with natural light. To eliminate harsh shadows, however, a special light is sometimes used.

An indoor shot for the brochure will show two men looking at pictures of food. Robert shows the men the positions he would like them to take for the photograph. Part of Robert's job is to make the photo an interesting one. Clients know Robert has good technical skills and will take a creative approach to his work.

When there will be people in the pictures, Robert must make them feel relaxed in front of the camera. A person who is uncomfortable will not look natural, and the photograph will not be acceptable. Robert's sense of humor is often helpful, and he has learned to be flexible—to change plans, if necessary, to solve a problem.

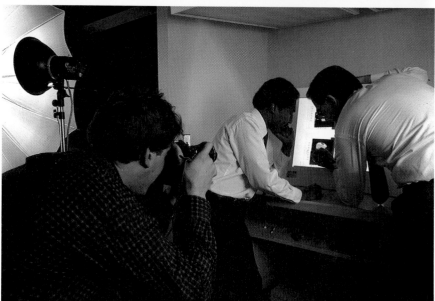

Robert will also photograph the food company's headquarters. He walks around the grounds with his client, looking at the building. He has to decide on the best angle from which to take the photograph. "Scouting" a location can take only a few minutes, or a full day or more. This client has limited time, so Robert must work quickly.

The position of the sun can create shadows that often add drama and excitement to outdoor photographs. Sometimes Robert can schedule his photo sessions to take advantage of shadows and other special effects with natural light. At other times, he must design a way to get a good shot in unfavorable conditions.

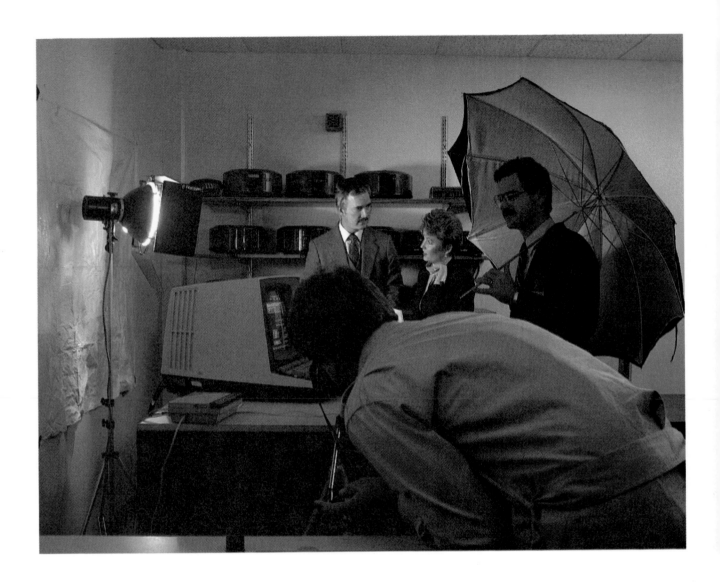

The next shot is a photo of a man and a woman standing near a computer. Robert puts an orange filter over one of his lights to add color to the photograph. His client holds an umbrella, to shield the computer screen from the lights. Otherwise the screen display will be overpowered by reflections.

The finished picture is an example of good commercial photography. By carefully positioning the elements in the shot, using creative lighting, and selecting the most appropriate lens and the best angle for the shot, Robert has been able to create an interesting photograph of an ordinary situation.

Another computer shot is needed for the same brochure, and Robert has to make sure the two pictures do not look too much alike. He decides to photograph a man reading a computer print-out, rather than standing near a computer screen. After he takes a Polaroid shot, Robert decides that the subject should remove his jacket.

Robert is still not satisfied with the shot. He makes an adjustment in the angle of his light and takes another Polaroid. He lets the subject have a look at the shot, too. Now he is ready to take the photograph. The final picture satisfies his critical eye and the needs of his client.

Sometimes Robert doesn't have the luxury of setting up a shot and trying out several ways of composing a photograph. On some locations he must stay as much in the background as possible. Often this means using a telephoto lens, which he can use to take a close-up shot from a distance.

Using his telephoto lens, Robert takes an on-the-job photograph of two electrical engineers without interrupting their work. He is satisfied with the angle he has finally worked out. The finished photograph will be a carefully edited portion of the view Robert sees around him. Making every situation look good is part of Robert's job.

For the last photograph of the day, Robert has designed a sunset shot, knowing the city lights will add drama. He arrives at the scene early to select the right angle and to make sure he is prepared to shoot when the light is just right. He chooses a magenta filter for the lens, to change the color of the pre-twilight sky.

Robert has set up the camera's tripod support, because he will be shooting exposures of longer than one second. He knows he will be happy with this shot. For Robert, working as a photographer makes every day a good one. The possibilities for interesting pictures are everywhere—at every time of day.